D0471365

Little People, BIG DREAMS

JOSEPHINE BAKER

Written by
Mª Isabel Sánchez Vegara

Illustrated by
Agathe Sorlet

Frances Lincoln
Children's Books

This is the incredible story of a girl
from St. Louis named Josephine.

Some would say she was born with nothing, but she had two legs made for dancing, a dazzling smile, and a free spirit—and she was going to use them.

When Josephine was a little girl,
white people seemed to live in another world.

They made all the rules—and these rules
were very different if your skin color was black.

But Josephine danced her way out of St. Louis and became a street artist. Then a theater performer. When Josephine moved, her legs were elastic fantastic!

Josephine traveled to New York and became the last dancer on the end of the chorus line.

But somehow everybody noticed her.
Her movements were silly and stylish at the same time.

Josephine knew that she had gone as far as a
black woman could go in America at that time. So,
when she was offered a job in a new show in Paris,
she jumped at the chance and sailed to Europe.

Here, black and white people lived alongside each other. For the first time in her life, Josephine felt free.

Josephine became a star overnight.
The shimmy, the moosh, the mess around, the
Charleston...all her movements were exciting.
People had never seen anything like it before.

First Paris, and then all of Europe...
Her fame grew and so did her pet collection!
She shared her life with cats, dogs, fish, birds,
a pig, a goat—and even a baby cheetah!
Her heart was big and full of love to give.

Josephine began singing and filming movies.
She was the first black woman to ever star in a film.
Her dazzling personality made her a total superstar!

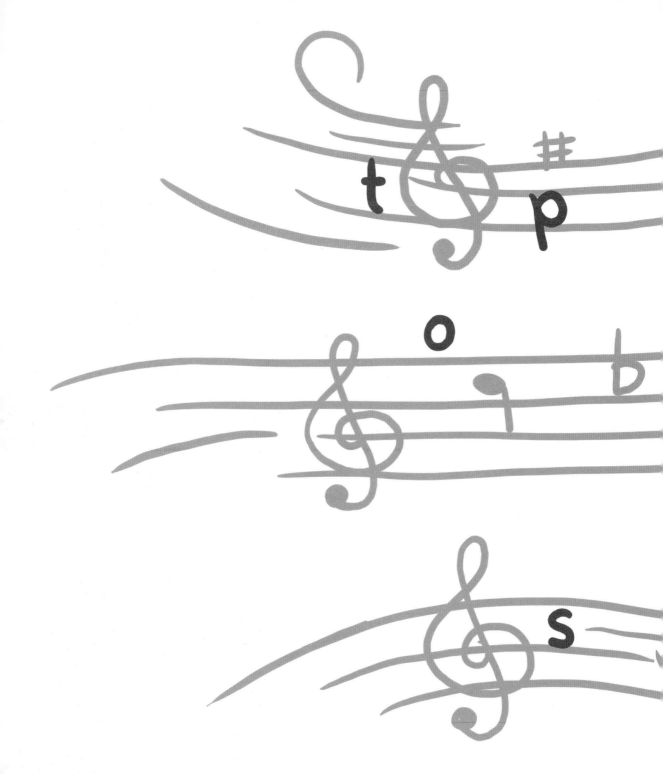

But then World War II began and half of Europe
was invaded. Josephine knew she had to do something.

She became a spy and smuggled secret reports in her music sheets. She was a heroine of the French Resistance!

When the war ended, Josephine adopted 12 children from the four corners of the globe. She believed people of all colors could live together in harmony and wanted to prove it to everyone.

But times were changing in America, and Josephine returned home. She traveled to Washington and marched for civil rights along with thousands of other people. A man named Dr. Martin Luther King Jr. marched with her.

And when she celebrated her fifty-year career onstage, the world gave her a standing ovation. It was a long way from St. Louis for little Josephine, but she had made it, in her own spectacular way.

JOSEPHINE BAKER

(Born 1906 • Died 1975)

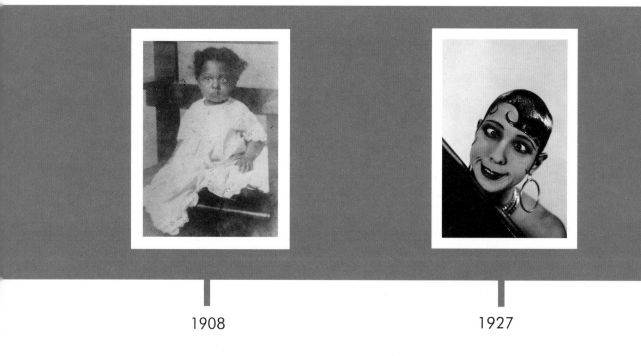

1908   1927

Josephine Baker was born Freda Josephine McDonald in St. Louis,
Missouri. Josephine's early years were difficult. She was brought
up in poverty in a segregated city. This meant there were separate
rules for white and black people. These rules affected everything:
from houses, medical care, and education to opportunites, jobs,
and access to services. Josephine made it despite the roadblocks
put in front of her. She honed her craft watching vaudeville
shows and danced herself out of the St. Louis slums. Her act was
acrobatic, improvised, and funny all at once. Her unique talent
took her to shows in Boston, New York, and Paris. And at the age
of 19, Josephine became an overnight sensation in her first Parisian

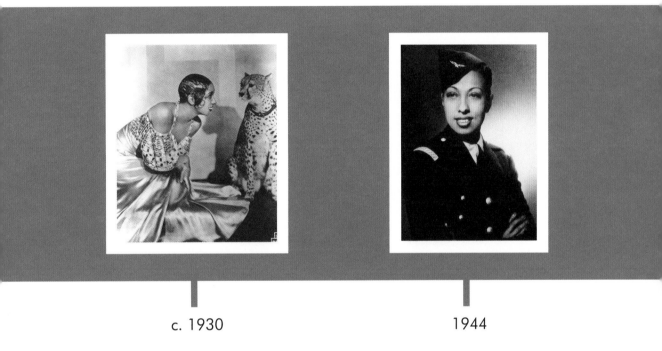

c. 1930

1944

show. Over the following years, she continued to amaze audiences onstage, famously wearing a banana skirt. She became the first black woman to star in a major film—going on to make four in total. Then, during World War II, Josephine worked as a spy, carrying information that helped the French Resistance against the Nazis. Josephine never stopped fighting for equal rights: she refused to perform in segregated theaters, she spoke at the March on Washington, and she adoped 12 children from around the world, calling them her "Rainbow Tribe." Her hope for the future was that people would learn to live in peace and without prejudice. She remained one of the biggest and brightest stars in entertainment for the rest of her life.

Want to find out more about **Josephine Baker?**
Read one of these great books:

Josephine by Patricia Hruby Powell and Christian Robinson
Jazz Age Josephine by Jonah Winter and Marjorie Priceman
Young, Gifted and Black by Jamia Wilson and Andrea Pippins
Little Leaders: Bold Women in Black History by Vashti Harrison

If you're in France, you could stop by Josephine's home, the Chateau des Milandes, to spot some of her most spectacular costumes.

Brimming with creative inspiration, how-to projects, and useful information to enrich your everyday life, Quarto Knows is a favorite destination for those pursuing their interests and passions. Visit our site and dig deeper with our books into your area of interest: Quarto Creates, Quarto Cooks, Quarto Homes, Quarto Lives, Quarto Drives, Quarto Explores, Quarto Gifts, or Quarto Kids.

Text © 2018 Mª Isabel Sánchez Vegara. Illustrations © 2018 Agathe Sorlet.

First Published in the UK in 2018 by Lincoln Children's Books, an imprint of The Quarto Group.

400 First Avenue North, Suite 400, Minneapolis, MN 55401, USA.

T (612) 344-8100 F (612) 344-8692 www.QuartoKnows.com

First Published in Spain in 2018 under the title Pequeña & Grande Josephine Baker

by Alba Editorial, s.l.u., Baixada de Sant Miquel, 1, 08002 Barcelona

www.albaeditorial.es

All rights reserved.

Published by arrangement with Alba Editorial, s.l.u. Translation rights arranged by IMC Agència Literària, SL

All rights reserved.

No part of this publication may be reproduced, stored in a retrieval system, or transmitted, in any form, or by any means, electrical, mechanical, photocopying, recording or otherwise without the prior written permission of the publisher or a license permitting restricted copying.

ISBN 978-1-78603-228-7

The illustrations were created digitally. Set in Futura BT.

Published by Rachel Williams • Designed by Karissa Santos and Sasha Moxon
Edited by Katy Flint • Production by Jenny Cundill

Manufactured in Guangdong, China CC042019

9 7 5 3 2 4 6 8

Photographic acknowledgments (pages 28–29, from left to right) 1. Josephine Baker, 1908 © ullstein bild via Getty Images 2. Josephine Baker, 1927 © George Hoyningen-Huene / Condé Nast via Getty Images 3. Josephine Baker, c. 1930 © Michael Ochs Archives / Getty Images 4. Portrait of Josephine Baker, 1944 © John D. Kisch / Separate Cinema Archive / Getty Images

Collect the Little People, BIG DREAMS series:

FRIDA KAHLO

ISBN: 978-1-84780-783-0

COCO CHANEL

ISBN: 978-1-84780-784-7

MAYA ANGELOU

ISBN: 978-1-84780-889-9

AMELIA EARHART

ISBN: 978-1-84780-888-2

AGATHA CHRISTIE

ISBN: 978-1-78603-220-1

MARIE CURIE

ISBN: 978-1-84780-962-9

ROSA PARKS

ISBN: 978-1-78603-018-4

AUDREY HEPBURN
ISBN: 978-1-78603-053-5

EMMELINE PANKHURST

ISBN: 978-1-78603-020-7

ELLA FITZGERALD
ISBN: 978-1-78603-087-0

ADA LOVELACE

ISBN: 978-1-78603-076-4

JANE AUSTEN
ISBN: 978-1-78603-120-4

GEORGIA O'KEEFFE
ISBN: 978-1-78603-122-8

HARRIET TUBMAN
ISBN: 978-1-78603-227-0

ANNE FRANK

ISBN: 978-1-78603-229-4

MOTHER TERESA

ISBN: 978-1-78603-230-0

JOSEPHINE BAKER

ISBN: 978-1-78603-228-7

L. M. MONTGOMERY
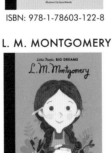

ISBN: 978-1-78603-233-1

JANE GOODALL
ISBN: 978-1-78603-231-7

SIMONE DE BEAUVOIR
ISBN: 978-1-78603-232-4

Now in board book format:

COCO CHANEL

ISBN: 978-1-78603-245-4

MAYA ANGELOU
ISBN: 978-1-78603-249-2

FRIDA KAHLO

ISBN: 978-1-78603-247-8

AMELIA EARHART

ISBN: 978-1-78603-251-5

MARIE CURIE
ISBN: 978-1-78603-253-9

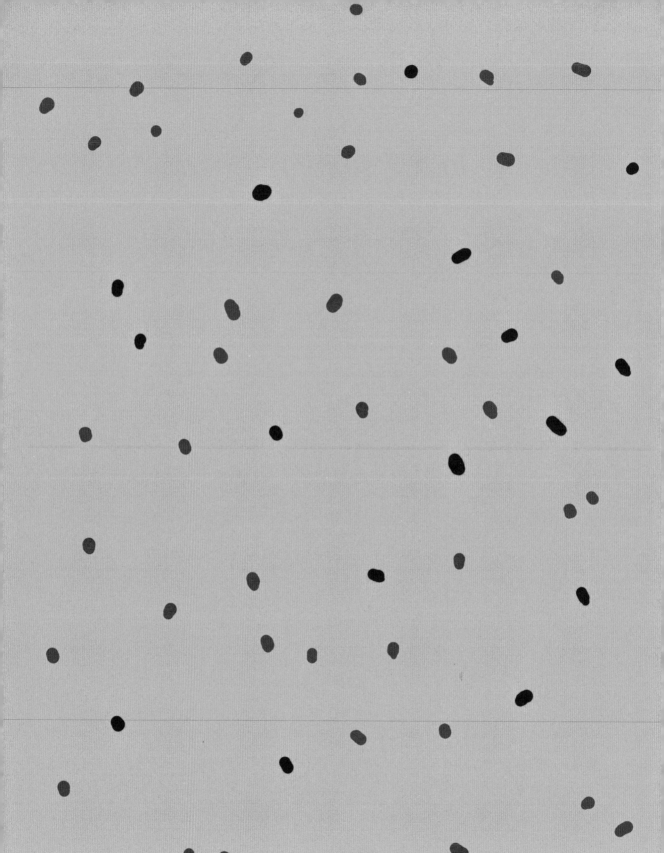